# Contents

# 1 The visit

This is a photograph of a class of schoolchildren like you.

One day their teacher said, "This term, Class 3, we are going to do a special project. It is about schooldays eighty years ago.

To start our project we shall spend a morning in the Victorian schoolroom at Armley Mills Museum. You will have to dress up like children in 1900. You will do the same lessons that they did. You will also have to behave like children in your great grandparents' day."

Armley Mills Industrial Museum

The Victorian schoolroom

The children were very excited. It would be like stepping
back in time.

This time-chart shows how far back they had to go.

Look at it carefully.

| 1900 | | 1930 | |
|---|---|---|---|

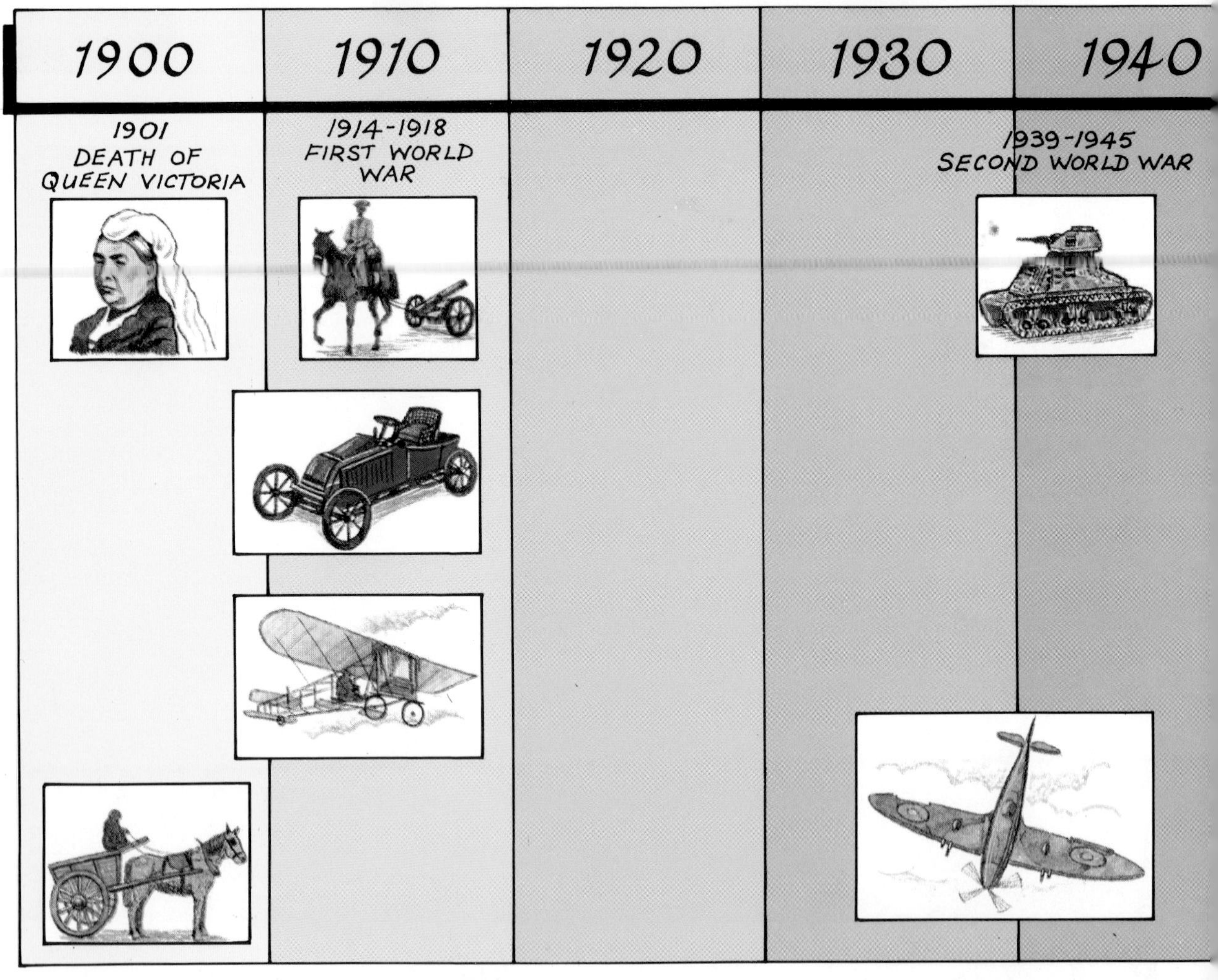

| 1900 | 1910 | 1920 | 1930 | 1940 |
|---|---|---|---|---|
| 1901 DEATH OF QUEEN VICTORIA | 1914-1918 FIRST WORLD WAR | | | 1939-1945 SECOND WORLD WAR |

- Which members of your family would have been children in 1900?
- Using the time-chart to help you, make a list of the ways in which their life was different from your life today.

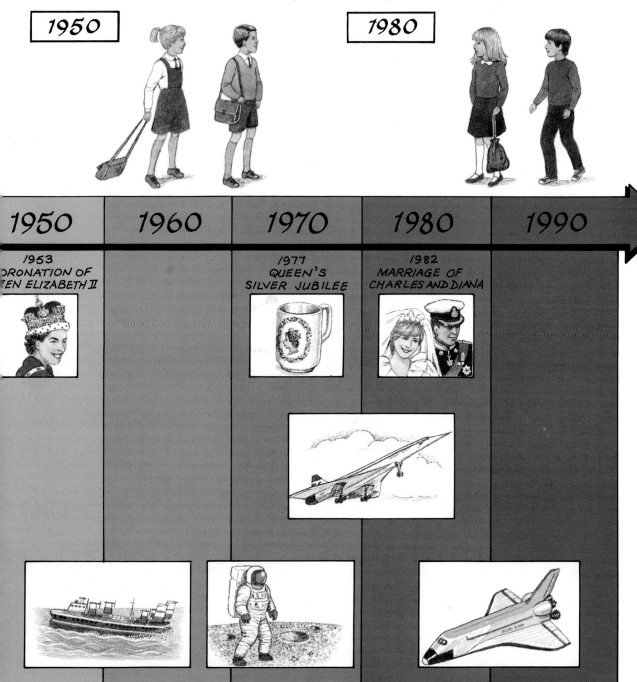

1950

1980

| 1950 | 1960 | 1970 | 1980 | 1990 |
|------|------|------|------|------|

1953
CORONATION OF
QUEEN ELIZABETH II

1977
QUEEN'S
SILVER JUBILEE

1982
MARRIAGE OF
CHARLES AND DIANA

# 2 Dressing up

At last the day came. The talking and planning were over. The children were ready to leave for the Victorian schoolroom. They had looked at photographs of schoolchildren in 1900 then tried to copy the clothes.

Royd's School, Rothwell, 1897

It's your turn now

Look at the old photograph.

1 How are the clothes of these children different from yours?

2 Why do you think the girls wore aprons?

3 Why did the boys wear big boots?

4 How did the children feel on a hot summer's day?

Now look at the photographs of Class 3.

5 Are all the children dressed up in the correct clothes?

# 3 Playing detectives

The children enjoyed their morning in the Victorian schoolroom. They soon discovered that school life was very different in 1900. Look at this photograph of the children in the schoolroom.

- In what ways is the schoolroom different from your classroom?

The time in the Victorian schoolroom went too quickly. Afterwards there were still lots of things the children wanted to know. "Can we find out more?" they asked. "We could do some detective work."

"Yes," replied their teacher. "You will have to look for clues. Then you can use these as evidence to tell you more about school life in 1900. But perhaps we should call you 'Time Detectives'. Ordinary detectives investigate today's mysteries. You will be trying to find out about things that happened eighty years ago."

Opposite are some of the clues the children found.

- What kinds of clues can you see?

In the rest of the book you will see what the Time Detectives found out about schooldays in 1900.

Laurie Lee
Cider With Rosie

ARMLEY ALBUM

LARK RISE TO CANDLEFORD
FLORA THOMPSON

BOOK

Lessons
cow cat bat
Horse lion Owl
animal Stag Bear Swallow
Kangaroo Squirrel Hen
Giraffe Herring Use

Tea Ferns Fruit
Vegetable Lefrs Ivy Wheat
Cocoa Carrot Callow

Moral { Honesty Courtesy
Kindness

249
Varied Occupations
Standard I
I
1 Geography
2 Drawing
3 Recitation
4 Musical Drill Marching
5 Natural History
6 Needlework
7 Singing
Lower Division
II
1 Building Bricklaying
2 Simple Conversational Lesson
3 Drawing Recitation
4 Needlework

Exercise Book.

# 4 Setting off

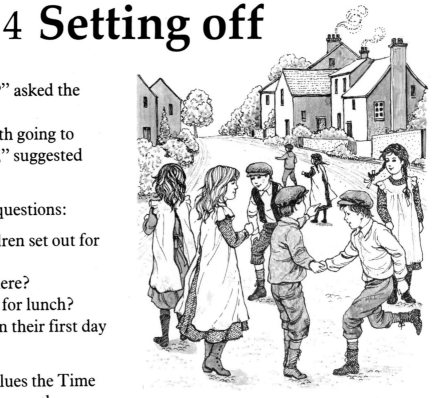

Country children on their way to school

"Where shall we start?" asked the Time Detectives.

"We could begin with going to school in the morning," suggested someone.

So they made a list of questions:

- What time did children set out for school in 1900?
- How did they get there?
- What did they have for lunch?
- How did they feel on their first day at school?

Here are some of the clues the Time Detectives found. They are the memories of people who were children in 1900.

❝ School began at 9 o'clock. We country children set out on our mile-and-a-half walk at 7 o'clock. We liked plenty of time to walk and play on the way. ❞

❝ The morning came without warning. My sisters tied my shoelaces, thrust a cap on my head and a baked potato in my pocket. I arrived just three feet tall. The playground roared. The potato burnt a hole in my pocket. The crowd came nearer. They began to prod me and spin me. They stole my potato. ❞

A school playground

A school cloakroom eighty years ago

❝ There were no school dinners. In good weather we went home to lunch. In bad weather we stayed. At 12 o'clock we were rushed into a small classroom. We sat on a bench with a mug of cocoa and a thick cheese sandwich. ❞

School dinners eighty years ago

❝ The cloakroom was wet with puddles, very damp and chilly. It was crammed with children fighting for a peg. I clung to my mother's hand, trembling with fear. ❞

**It's your turn now**

1 Write down answers to the Time Detectives' questions about 1900.

2 Now ask the same questions about going to school today.

3 Use your findings to make bar charts.

4 In what ways was going to school different in 1900 when your great grandparents were children?

5 Write down your memories of your own first day at school. How did you feel?

# 5 The school

The classroom visited by the children was inside a museum. But the Time Detectives wanted to know what a real Victorian school looked like.

They found two drawings of schools eighty years ago. Here they are. Look at them carefully.

A town school

## A town school
This was built for large numbers of children. Sometimes over a thousand children went to school there.

❛ The school was as large as a fortress, its plain brick front broken by large windows which let plenty of light into the classroom. ❜

## A village school

This school had only one classroom. All the children were taught in the same classroom. There were often only forty-five children at the school.

A village school

6 It was a small building. There was no water laid on. It had earth closets. [This means that the toilets were just holes dug in the ground.] The water supply was in a small bucket which was filled every morning. 9

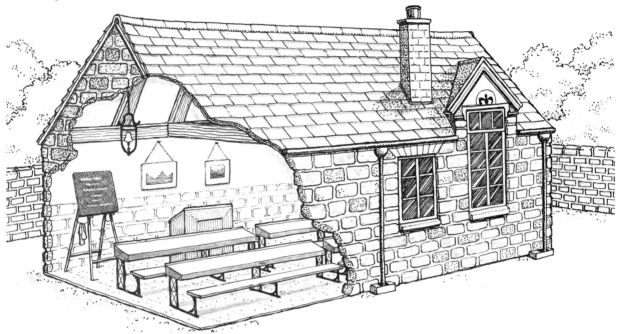

It's your turn now

1 How was the town school different from the village school?

2 How were these schools different from your school today?

Copy and fill in a grid like the one below.

3 Try to find out when your school was built.

| Think about: | Schools in 1900 | My school today |
|---|---|---|
| the building<br>the classrooms<br>the playground<br>the toilets | | |

# 6 Starting the day

Morning assembly

The Time Detectives discovered that school began in the same way each morning for children in 1900.

❝ Assembly was taken by the headmaster in the hall. We had prayers every morning, a hymn and lessons in Scripture. We learned to repeat parrot-wise the Lord's Prayer, the 23rd Psalm and the story of Samuel. ❞

Then the headmaster and teachers inspected all the children.

❝ You daren't be late. There was always an inspection in the morning to see that you were clean and smart. The girls always used to have clean white pinnies [aprons]. ❞

### A child's morning prayer
*I thank thee, Lord, for the quiet rest,*
*and for the care of me,*
*Oh let me through the day be blest,*
*and kept from harm by thee,*
*Help me to please my parents dear,*
*and do whatever they tell;*
*Bless all my friends, both far and near,*
*and keep them safe and well.*

❛ Every Friday the teacher used to say "when you come back on Monday, let's have you with your boots cleaned and a nice clean collar. And remember to wash your neck." ❜

Afterwards the children marched off to their classroom. Sometimes they sang this rhyme:

**Marching rhyme**
*We march to our places,*
*With clean hands and faces,*
*And pay great attention*
*    to all we are told.*
*For we know we shall never*
*    be happy and clever,*
*But learning is better*
*    than silver and gold.*

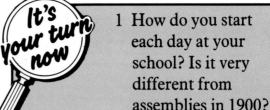

It's your turn now

1 How do you start each day at your school? Is it very different from assemblies in 1900?

2 Why do you think teachers wanted the children to be so clean?

3 Try to learn the prayer and the marching rhyme parrot-wise.

Are you clean?

# 7 Reading and 'Rithmetic

A reading lesson in Great Grandma's day

The Time Detectives discovered that the most important lessons were reading, writing and arithmetic. This is a photograph of a reading lesson eighty years ago. First the class pointed to a word in their books. Then they all read it aloud at the same time.

Later they read stories like this:

### The boy and the nettle
*Two boys were playing in the fields. When one of them struck the ball into a bed of nettles, the other ran to get it, and was badly stung. Crying with pain, he went to his mother. "You should have been more careful," said she, "and no harm would have come to you." "But, mother," he replied, "I hardly touched the nettle." "That is just it," she said. "If you touch a nettle gently it will sting you, but if you grasp it firmly it will not hurt you."*
Moral: *Boldly face a difficulty or a danger if you wish to overcome it.*

(*from* My Book of Fables, *c. 1895*)

At their own school, the Time Detectives had started a new Maths book. There were lots of interesting puzzles and coloured pictures. Everyone worked at their own speed. They got a shock when they had their arithmetic lesson in the Victorian schoolroom. It was just like the lessons remembered by these children eighty years ago.

6 Throughout the morning we chanted out tables. Passers-by could hear our voices. We rocked to our chanting. Twice two are four, twice three are six .... 9

Class 3 testing tables

6 We learned how many gallons of water would stay in a fifty-gallon bath with three holes in and both taps running full. It didn't matter that we had no baths at home. 9

$$\begin{array}{r} 5\,2\,4\,7\,1\,0\,2\,1 \\ 3 \\ \hline 1\,5\,7\,4\,1\,3\,0\,6\,3 \end{array}$$

A child's book – multiplication sums

It's your turn now

1 How is the reading lesson and the story different from yours?

2 How are the arithmetic lessons different from yours?

# 8 Writing

During their morning in the schoolroom, the children had a writing lesson.

First the teacher showed them how to make their letters by drawing pot hooks. These were lines with hooks at the top or loops at the bottom. The children had to copy them again and again.

At first they did not use paper. They had a little tray filled with sand. They made letters in sand, using their fingers. To rub out the letters, they shook the sand.

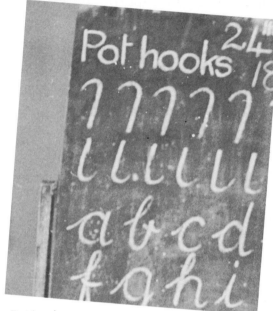

Pot hooks

Writing in sand

After this they wrote on slate with a slate pencil. It made a horrible squeaking noise. To rub out, the children brought their own sponge in a tin. The naughty ones used their sleeves.

Writing with a slate and pencil

In 1900 only older children were allowed to use ink.

❝ Once we could draw letters, we learned to write in copperplate. The ink was made from powder by adding water. Each morning little ink-wells were filled by a monitor [one of the children, chosen to do this special job]. The pens had steel nibs and wooden holders. Special paper was used. Small letters fit into one square, capitals into two. No one was allowed to use their left hand. ❞

Below, you can see some copperplate writing.

Pen and paper

*Quick at speech, slow at work.*

Inkpot and powder

It's your turn now

1 Why do you think little children in 1900 learned to write with sand trays and slates instead of paper and pencils?

2 Why do you think only older children were allowed to use ink?

3 Ask your teacher to give you a Victorian writing lesson. Begin by doing pot hooks. Then try to copy the copperplate handwriting.

4 Why do you think everyone had to use their right hand?

# 9 Pick up your dumb-bells

At the schoolroom, the Time Detectives had a drill lesson. Here are some clues to show you what they did.

❛ We were lined up in neat rows. The teacher gave the orders. "ATTENTION", "ARMS BEND". In bad weather we did drill between the desks. And in good weather, outside in the playground. ❜

Class 3 picking up their dumb-bells

Dumb-bells

A class of boys at drill in 1900

Girls at drill, 1900

### Why do drill?

*Children who do drill,*
*Seldom are ill,*
*Seldom look pale,*
*Delicate and frail,*
*Seldom are sulky and*
*Seldom are spiteful*
*But always delightful.*
*So dears, I still*
*Beg you to drill.*
(Jennet Humphrey,
*Laugh and Learn*, 1890)

Infants at drill, 1900

It's your turn now

1 a Why were the children made to do drill?
  b Do you think it worked?

2 In the rhyme, what does the word "seldom" mean?

3 What lessons do you have instead of drill?

4 How are your PE lessons different from drill?

5 Ask your teacher to give you a drill lesson. It should last at least thirty minutes.

# 10 **Girls only**

The Time Detectives found out a lot about morning lessons in 1900. "But what did children do in the afternoon?" they wondered. They discovered that sometimes girls and boys did different things. Here are some clues about special lessons for girls.

6 The girls in my class were making pinafores for themselves, putting in tiny stitches and biting off their cotton like grown-up women. 9

6 We were taught to sweep, dust, polish, make beds, bath a baby doll, wash and iron. 9

A girls' laundry lesson

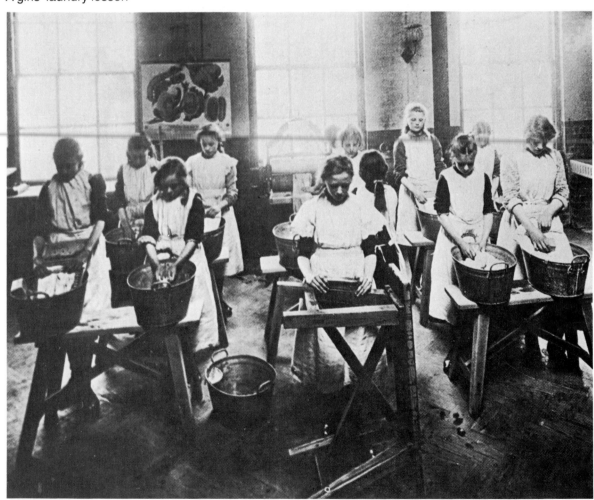

A girls' cookery lesson

Dinners for one Week
Sunday. Joint, cabbage, potatoes,
Yorkshire Pudding, apple pie
Monday. Cold meat, fried potatoes,
Rice pudding,
Tuesday. Soup and dumplings, Jam
roly-poly.
Wednesday.Fish, potatoes, sauce, Sprouts,
sago Pudding.
Thursday. Fish cakes, potatoes, Bread
and Butter pudding.
Friday. Liver, fried onions, bacon,
roasted potatoes, Cheese and
bread.
Saturday Steak and Kidney Pie,
potatoes, Blancmange, and
jam.

9. 2. 05

*It's your turn now*

1  How was wash-day in 1900 different from today?

2  The girls were told to make a quick and easy dinner on wash-day. Can you think why?

3  Look at the menu. Which day do you think was wash-day?

4  Do a survey to find out if your dinners are the same as or different from those in the past.

5  What jobs do you think girls did when they grew up?

6  Have girls' jobs changed since 1900? Give reasons for your answer.

# 11 Boys only

In Great Grandma's time, girls learnt how to be wives and mothers. But what special lessons did boys have? The Time Detectives found these clues. Look at them carefully.

## Country boys eighty years ago

❝ In the afternoons girls learned sewing together. The boys did more sums or writing. Just the sort of thing they had been doing all morning. They tried to see what we were making. They were very naughty. They kept forgetting which sums they were doing or spelling words wrongly. ❞

❝ When the girls were doing needlework, the boys would open their books for silent reading. When the boys had to do a bit of carpentry, the girls would have their turn at silent reading. ❞

A long afternoon

## Town boys eighty years ago

6 Once a week we were taken from school to a special centre. We learnt to do woodwork and metalwork – things which would help us in later life. 9

A woodwork lesson

It's your turn now

1 Why do you think the country boys were naughty?

2 Why were girls not allowed to do lessons such as woodwork and metalwork in 1900?

3 What jobs did boys expect to do when they grew up in 1900?

4 What job do you hope to do when you grow up?

5 Have boys' jobs changed since 1900? Give reasons for your answer.

6 If you had been a child in 1900, would you have wanted to be a boy or a girl? Give reasons for your choice.

# 12 Being good

Class 3 being seen but not heard

In the Victorian schoolroom, the children had to be very quiet and well-behaved.

"Were teachers always so strict eighty years ago?" they asked. They soon discovered that in the past, children had to be seen but not heard.

❛ The teachers were really strict. They would throw chalk at you or the board rubber. ❜

❛ You did as you were told because you were scared of the teachers. ❜

❛ I don't think you noticed how strict school was. Everyone was strict. If our father was speaking, we would never dare interrupt him. ❜

❛ Miss Higgs could not control her class. They hid her cane and put frogs in her desk. The girls were as bad as the boys. Miss Shepherd ruled by love and kindness. ❜

As well as these memories, the Time Detectives found an old punishment book. Here are some of the children who were punished:

**Castleton Primary School, Leeds, Punishment Book, 1904**

| | | | |
|---|---|---|---|
| 8 Oct. | William Frazer | Thumping a girl | 2 strokes on hand |
| 16 Oct. | Albert Whitehead | Lazy and dirty | 2 strokes on hand |
| 6 Nov. | Arthur Parker | Bad behaviour | 2 strokes on hand |

Sometimes children had to learn rhymes like this:

***You will never be sorry***
*For using gentle words,*
*For doing your best,*
*For being kind to the poor,*
*For looking before leaping,*
*For thinking before speaking,*
*For doing what you can to make*
*others happy.*

*It's your turn now*

1 What kinds of things were children punished for in 1900?

2 What kind of children did teachers like?

3 What did children think about their teachers?

4 Were teachers the only people who were strict with children in 1900?

5 Were all teachers strict?

The Cane

# 13 The school-yard

"We know a lot about lessons in our great grandparents' time," said the children. "What about playtime? What games did they play?" Look at these pictures of children's games eighty years ago.

❝ There was not always a ball to be had, for the smallest rubber ball cost a penny. Pennies were scarce. Boys would kick an old tin can about for a football. ❞

**Dipping rhyme**

*One, two, three, four, five, six, seven,*
*All good children go to heaven,*
*Penny on the water,*
*Tuppence on the sea,*
*Three pence on the railway*
*Out goes she.*

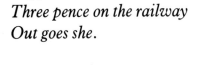

It's your turn now

1 How many games can you name?

2 Why did boys not play football very often?

3 How many of these games do children still play today?

# 14 The Day of Judgement

During the morning in the schoolroom, the teacher talked about the inspector. She said the children must learn their lessons well before the school inspector's visit. He would test their reading, writing and arithmetic. Also he inspected the children's drill and the girls' needlework. The results were important to the school. The inspector decided how much money the school would get to buy books and other things.

The children wondered what an inspector's visit was like. Here are one girl's memories of an inspector's visit.

Children on the way to school

The inspector calls

## Laura's story

"The Inspector of Schools came once a year. There was no singing or quarrelling on the way to school that morning. The children, in their clean pinafores and blackened boots, walked deep in thought. Some years he would come in the morning. Others in the afternoon. So after prayers, the children settled down for a long wait. Ten, eleven, the hands of the clock dragged on!

At last came the sound of wheels crunching on the gravel. Classes came out to read, others bent over their sums. The composition class made a hash of their letters. The children had been told beforehand that they must fill one page, so they wrote in very large handwriting and spaced their lines well.

At last it was over! No one would know who had passed for a fortnight, but that did not trouble the children at all. They crept like mice out of the school, but once out of sight, what shouting and skipping took place!"

## Inspector's report

"This is a very good school. It is a cheerful place to be. The lessons are good and the children have done well in their exams."

After the inspection

*It's your turn now*

1 a How did the children feel before the inspector came?
  b How do you know?

2 a How did they feel after he had gone?
  b How do you know?

3 Do you still have inspectors' visits in your school today?

4 Look at the inspector's report. Why did he like this school?

# 15 The infant class

An infant class in Great Grandma's day

The children found their lessons in the Victorian schoolroom were hard.

"What was it like in the infant class?" asked one of the Time Detectives. "Were their lessons different from the kind of thing we did in Class 1?" Here is some of the evidence they found.

❛ The infant room was packed with toys I had never seen before – coloured shapes and balls of clay, stuffed birds and men to paint. Also there was a frame of counting beads. ❜

❛ We were taught to knit. We cut shapes of paper, played with clay and made pictures with chalk, pencil and water paint. ❜

❛ I learnt to cut out men from paper, chalk sums on my slate, make snakes from crayons and write my name in large and small letters. ❜

*It's your turn now*

1 Make a list of the activities in the infant class in 1900.

2 Did you do the same sorts of things in your infant class?

3 If you had been a school child eighty years ago would you have preferred the infant class or the junior classes? Give reasons for your answer.

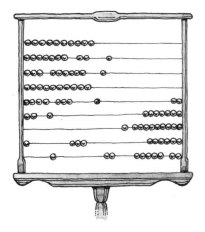

Abacus counting frame

Soft toys

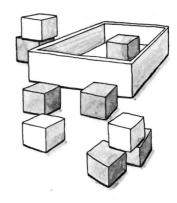

Bricks

Paints and brushes

Wash-day

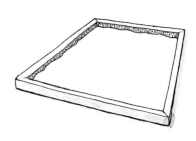

Clay tray

Teaset

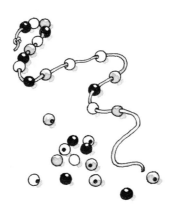

Bead-threading

Clay bin

# 16 Out and about

Do you enjoy visits out of school? The children enjoyed their visit to the Victorian schoolroom. It was exciting to dress up and step back to a different time in a different place. They wondered if children eighty years ago had trips out of school.

Look at these memories of children and teachers.

A school visit to the seaside

6 We had nature-study. On Tuesday afternoons we explored the fields and examined the hedges, trees and flowers. We came back to the classroom with plants to draw on our slates. 9

6 We kept records of the date of picking the first primrose or seeing the first swallow. 9

6 We had a card today inviting the children to the Leeds Flower Show. The cost will be one penny. 9

6 On May Day we had a grand tea in the school after the crowning of the May Queen and dancing round the Maypole. 9

6 Yesterday the children should have had their annual trip to Kirkstall Abbey. The weather changed suddenly so the trip was delayed. 9

6 Nearly half the schoolchildren in Leeds have visited the museum. They come in groups of 250. They listen to a lantern slide lecture. Then, in small groups, they are taken round the museum. 9

*It's your turn now*

1 What kinds of school visits did children make eighty years ago?

2 Are they the same as the kinds of school visits you make?

3 Can you spot any differences?

A museum visit

May Day

A school picnic

A nature ramble

# 17 Rewards for the few

A prizegiving

During their investigations, the Time Detectives found many things which puzzled them. One of them was this photograph. It shows a prizegiving.

Some of the pupils had been given medals. At other schools pupils were given books or certificates.

Attendance certificate

Attendance medal

A prize certificate from inside a book

- Look at the prizes on this page. What were they for?

Could you work it out? The prizes were given partly for good behaviour.

But they were also given for "good attendance". This means never missing a day at school for at least a year.

"Why did pupils get prizes for just going to school?" asked the children. Their teacher told them that in 1900 many children spent a lot of time off school. "This worried their headmasters," she continued. "The children fell behind with their lessons and would find it hard to do the exams when the inspector called."

This interested the Time Detectives. They decided to try to find out why so many children stayed away from school in 1900. In sections 18 and 19 (pages 38–41) you will see some of the evidence they discovered.

# 18 Coughs and sneezes

Their teacher showed the Time Detectives some pages from old school diaries. These diaries were called log-books. In their log-books, headteachers wrote down important happenings in their schools each day. Here are some of the things headteachers in and near Leeds wrote about their schools.

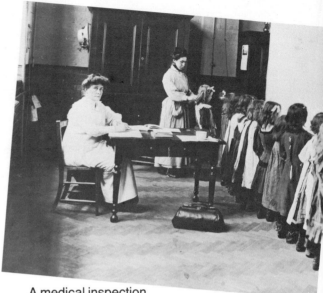
A medical inspection

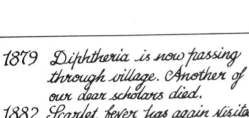

1879 Diphtheria is now passing through village. Another of our dear scholars died.

1882 Scarlet fever has again visited the village. Many children absent.

1882 A.P. absent — no shoes.

1884 Sixty-nine girls are absent from fever, measles, bad eyes, nits, ringworm. I sent home three because they were filthy.

1886 Many girls come half-clothed and half-fed. The food they get is chiefly tea and dry bread.

1886 The fever spreads rapidly. Some children have died.

1909 The vicar took four children to Leeds Infirmary to have eyesight tested. They are poor children. Their parents cannot pay doctor's fees.

Poor children without shoes

Poor housing in Leeds

Poor children queuing for breakfast

*It's your turn now*

Look at the photographs and the log-book.

1 What illnesses kept children away from school a hundred years ago?

2 Which illnesses were the most dangerous for children?

3 Why do you think so many children had these illnesses in the past?

4 Do a survey to find out what illnesses kept children in your class away from school last year.

5 How many of your illnesses are the same as illnesses a hundred years ago?

6 Why do you think you are healthier than children a hundred years ago?

# 19 Little workers

One of the Time Detectives found more evidence about staying away from school. It was in an old punishment book.

**1901, Armley Primary School, Punishment Book**

| Date | Scholar's Name | Offence | Punishment |
|------|----------------|---------|------------|
| Jan 15. | Edith Maurice | Truanting and lying | 2 strokes on hand |
| Jan 15. | Minnie Maurice | Truanting and lying | 2 strokes on hand |

"These children must have been doing something important," said another of the Time Detectives. "I wouldn't risk getting caned for nothing."

Next they looked at some pages from old school log-books. Here are some of the things one headmaster wrote about his pupils.

**Aberford Church of England School**

| 1898 | 15th June | John Walton marked absent. He has been working all year and is not yet 13. |
| | 2nd July | Pea-pulling five miles off. Few children at school. |
| 1899 | 26th April | Many girls absent. This is washing day. |
| | 19th June | Few children at school. Turnip~thinning has started. |
| 1900 | 2nd Nov. | Ten boys away all day beating bushes at Hazelwood for a gentleman who takes the shooting. |

A family making brushes

A shoeshine boy

Boy washing step

Children at work in the fields

*It's your turn now*

Look carefully at the picture and the headmaster's comments.

1 Why do you think children were kept at home to help with the washing?

2 Why do you think so many children were kept off school to do other work?

3 How important do you think school was to children in 1900? Give reasons for your answer.

# 20 Then and now

The children enjoyed their project about schooldays in the past. They discovered that life had been different when their great grandparents were children. Many things about school had changed since 1900. A few things were still the same.

**It's your turn now**

Look at the pictures on the opposite page. They show some objects from schools eighty years ago.

1 Can you remember what children did with each of them?

2 Do you still have these objects in your school today?

3 If not, what do you have instead?

4 Copy and complete a chart like this, to show your findings:

5 In what ways has school changed since 1900?

6 What things are still the same?

7 Do you wish you had been a schoolchild eighty years ago?

8 What would you have liked about being a schoolchild eighty years ago?

9 What would you have disliked about being a schoolchild eighty years ago?

| School in 1900 | | | My school today |
|---|---|---|---|
| Object | What is it? | What was it for? | Do we still have this today? |
| 1 2 3 etc. | Slate | Children learned to write with this | No. Today we use pencils or pens, and paper. |

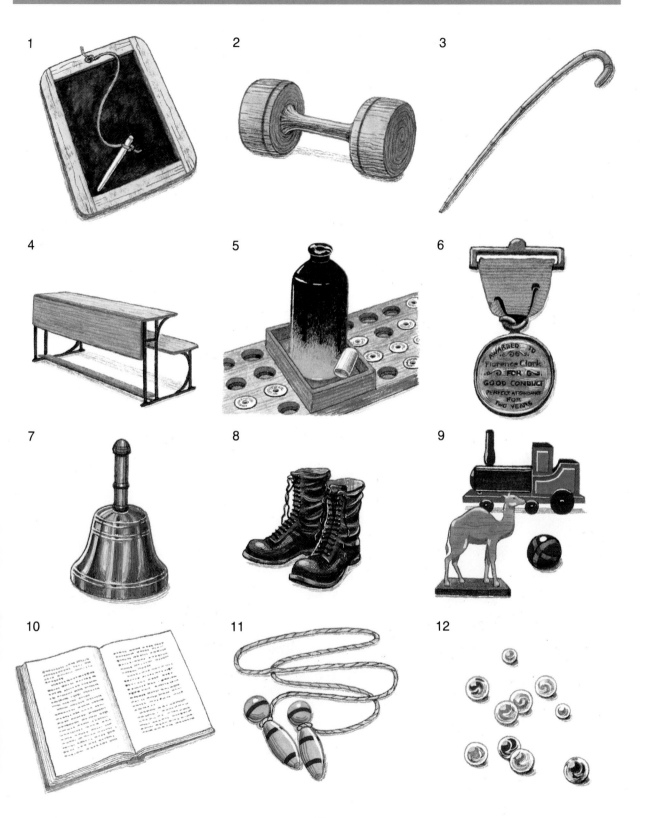

1

2

3

4

5

6

7

8

9

10

11

12

# 21 Asking "why?"

The Time Detectives liked looking at evidence about Great Grandma's schooldays. They discovered many differences between then and now. They also had lots of questions about why people did things differently then.

Here are some of the things that puzzled the children. Look at the pictures and the questions. Can you think of any answers?

The Time Detectives took colour photographs of their visit to the schoolroom. Why were old photographs black and white or brown and white, not colour?

Why did the children have to learn so many things off by heart?

Why did children use slates and slate pencils instead of felt-tip pens and paper?

Why were teachers stricter in the past?

Why did children wear strong boots or clogs instead of shoes or trainers?

What did children feel about going to school in the past?

# 22 Doing your own project

Perhaps you would like to do your own project about school life
in the past. You will have to play at being Time Detectives too.

1  Find clues and evidence about school life.

2  Make a list of questions you would like to ask.

What was the school like?

What lessons did children have?

How did children feel about going to school?

How was school different?

What things have changed?

What things are still the same?

3  Use your evidence to work out answers to your questions.

4  Make a scrapbook of your discoveries.

School life in 1900

toys

good conduct and attendance medal

ink

writing

clothes

boy's cap

boy

girl

boot

# Acknowledgements

The author and publishers wish to acknowledge the following photograph sources:

Armley Mills Industrial Museum, pages 3 (bottom), 23 (bottom), 37 (bottom); Barnaby's Picture Library, page 41 (top right), BBC Hulton Picture Library, pages 9, 25, 32, 34, 35 (middle top), 35 (middle bottom), 35 (bottom), 39; Illustration of a cross section of a school by Peter North reproduced from History Not So Long Ago (Autumn 1979) with permission of BBC Enterprises, page 12; Beamish North of England Open Air Museum, page 45 (bottom); Fawcett Library, page 22; Greater London Council, pages 16, 21 (top), 38; J. Grey Collection/Hitchen, pages 17 (top), 19 (middle), 37 (top); Leeds City Library, pages 14, 20 (bottom); Leeds City Museum, Mr P. Brears, page 35 (top); London Residuary Body, pages 18 (bottom left), 21 (bottom); C. E. Makepeace, page 41 (bottom left); Aileen Plummer, pages 2, 8, 44; J. Plummer, pages 18 (bottom right), 23 (top), 36; Salvation Army, pages 11, 38/39 (bottom), 41 (top left); John Topham Picture Library, page 48 (bottom right); F. Watkinson, John Taylor Teachers Centre, pages 19 (top), 19 (bottom), 20 (top left); F. D. Welch, pages 7, 17 (bottom), 18 (top), 20 (top right), 26, 45 (top left).

The author and publishers wish to thank the following who have kindly given permission for the use of copyright material:

Leeds Local Education Authority for extracts from Leeds School Log Books; Oxford University Press for extracts from *Lark Rise to Candleford* by Flora Thompson, 1945.

The author and publishers also wish to thank the staff and children of Roundhay Church of England School, Leeds, and in particular Mrs Wales, for their help in the making of this book.

Cover photograph J. Plummer

The publishers have made every effort to trace all the copyright holders, but where they have failed to do so they will be pleased to make the necessary arrangements at the first opportunity.

First published by Macmillan Education Ltd 1988

Published by
**Thomas Nelson and Sons Ltd**
Nelson House   Mayfield Road
Walton-on-Thames   Surrey
KT12 5PL   UK

NPN 9 8 7 6 5 4 3

ISBN 0-17-425066-5

Illustrated by Anna Hancock
Cover illustration David Dowland and Joyce Smith
Design by Sylvia Tate

Printed in Hong Kong

British Library Cataloguing in Publication Data
Morgan, Jean,
Great grandma's schooldays.—(Time Detectives).
1. Readers—1950
I. Title  II. Series
   428.6  PE1119
   ISBN 0-333-38841-0 (Macmillan)